MATH MASTERS · ANALYZE THIS!

Patterns

Claire Piddock

Educational Media

rourkeeducationalmedia.com

Before Reading:

Building Academic Vocabulary and Background Knowledge

Before reading a book, it is important to tap into what your child or students already know about the topic. This will help them develop their vocabulary, increase their reading comprehension, and make connections across the curriculum.

1. Look at the cover of the book. What will this book be about?
2. What do you already know about the topic?
3. Let's study the Table of Contents. What will you learn about in the book's chapters?
4. What would you like to learn about this topic? Do you think you might learn about it from this book? Why or why not?
5. Use a reading journal to write about your knowledge of this topic. Record what you already know about the topic and what you hope to learn about the topic.
6. Read the book.
7. In your reading journal, record what you learned about the topic and your response to the book.
8. After reading the book complete the activities below.

Content Area Vocabulary

Read the list. What do these words mean?

coordinate plane
core
even numbers
geometric
odd numbers
ordered pairs
pattern
repeating pattern
term

After Reading:

Comprehension and Extension Activity

After reading the book, work on the following questions with your child or students in order to ch their level of reading comprehension and content mastery.

1. What is the difference between dividing even numbers and odd numbers? (Summarize)
2. Explain what a repeating pattern is. (Infer)
3. How do you find patterns in a multiplication table? (Asking questions)
4. Describe a pattern rule. (Text to self connection)
5. How can you compare two patterns? (Asking questions)

Extension Activity

Practice all the concepts in the book to master patterns!

Table of Contents

Even and Odd

Partners are even. They come in twos!
Divide **even numbers** by 2 and there will be
0 left over.

Even numbers end with
0, 2, 4, 6, or 8.

Odd numbers are like partners plus 1.
Divide odd numbers by 2, and there will be
1 left over.

Odd numbers end with
1, 3, 5, 7, or 9.

Which numbers are even? Which numbers are odd?

440

508 23

128 99

125

Answers:
Even: 128, 440, 508
Odd: 23, 99, 125

What are Patterns?

A **pattern** is something that repeats using some rule that you can describe.

The rule for even numbers is:

Start with 0. Add 2. Repeat adding 2.

The pattern is

0, 2, 4, 6, 8, 10, 12, 14, . . .

The rule for odd numbers is—you guessed it—

Start with 1. Add 2. Repeat adding 2.

The pattern is

1, 3, 5, 7, 9, 11, 13, . . .

You can make up all kinds of patterns.

Here's one.

Start with 10. Add 3. Repeat adding 3.

The pattern is

10, 13, 16, 19, 22, . . .

Here is another kind of pattern.

1, 2, 3, 1, 2, 3, 1, 2, 3, . . .

This pattern is easier to describe in words:

Count 1, 2, 3 and repeat.

Shape Patterns

You might see patterns without numbers.
The pattern shown below is a **repeating pattern**.

A pattern rule tells how to build a pattern. The
core of a pattern is the smallest part that repeats.

What is the smallest part of the pattern above
that repeats?

the cat and the dog

The core of the pattern above is

What animal comes next?

This is a repeating shape pattern.

What is the smallest part of the pattern that repeats?

One x and two hearts.

The core is

What 3 shapes come next?

What is the core of this pattern?

A B C A B C A B C . . .

What are the next 4 letters in the pattern?

Shape and Number Patterns

Shape patterns can be related to number patterns. Count the squares to figure out the number pattern.

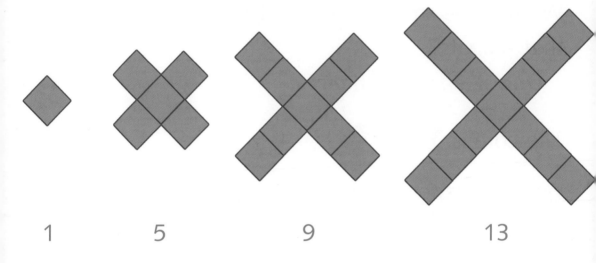

1   5   9   13

Add a square to each end of the X to continue the pattern.

The pattern rule is

Start with 1. Repeat adding 4.

In this pattern, count the lines in each figure.

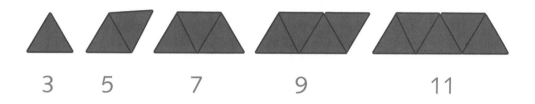

3   5   7   9   11

Add a triangle to continue.

The pattern rule is
    Start with 3.
    Repeat adding 2.

What is the next
number in the pattern?

Hidden Patterns

Find patterns in the addition table. Look at the shaded diagonal squares.

+	0	1	2	3	4	5	6	7	8	9	10
0	0	1	2	3	4	5	6	7	8	9	10
1	1	2	3	4	5	6	7	8	9	10	11
2	2	3	4	5	6	7	8	9	10	11	12
3	3	4	5	6	7	8	9	10	11	12	13
4	4	5	6	7	8	9	10	11	12	13	14
5	5	6	7	8	9	10	11	12	13	14	15
6	6	7	8	9	10	11	12	13	14	15	16
7	7	8	9	10	11	12	13	14	15	16	17
8	8	9	10	11	12	13	14	15	16	17	18
9	9	10	11	12	12	14	15	16	17	18	19
10	10	11	12	13	14	15	16	17	18	19	20

The orange numbers show a repeating pattern, but the number stays the same.

10, 10, 10, 10, . . .

The pattern rule is: Begin at 10. Repeat adding 10.

The blue numbers show a pattern of numbers that increase.

3, 5, 7, 9, 11, . . .

The pattern rule is: Begin at 3. Repeat adding 2.

Look at the addition table again. All the diagonals that slope up to the right repeat the same number. All the diagonals that slope down from the left show adding 2.

Other patterns in the table do not result in a list of numbers, but you can describe them. In the yellow squares, the diagonals have the same sum.

+	0	1	2	3	4	5	6	7	8	9	10
0	0	1	2	3	4	5	6	7	8	9	10
1	1	2	3	4	5	6	7	8	9	10	11
2	2	3	4	5	6	7	8	9	10	11	12
3	3	4	5	6	7	8	9	10	11	12	13
4	4	5	6	7	8	9	10	11	12	13	14
5	5	6	7	8	9	10	11	12	13	14	15
6	6	7	8	9	10	11	12	13	14	15	16
7	7	8	9	10	11	12	13	14	15	16	17
8	8	9	10	11	12	13	14	15	16	17	18
9	9	10	11	12	12	14	15	16	17	18	19
10	10	11	12	13	14	15	16	17	18	19	20

What are the sums of the diagonals in each yellow square above?

3 + 5 = ? and 4 + 4 = ?

9 + 11 = ? and 10 + 10 = ?

7 + 9 = ? and 8 + 8 = ?

16 + 18 = ? and 17 + 17 = ?

34, 34

16, 16

20, 20

8, 8

Find patterns in the multiplication table below. Look across any row or down any column to see the pattern of multiples for each number. You might call it the times table for the numbers.

2, 4, 6, 8, ...

3, 6, 9, 12, ...

4, 8, 12, 16, ...

There's a hidden pattern in the digits of the numbers that are shaded in yellow. The sum of the digits of each multiple equals 9.

1 + 8 = 9;   2 + 7 = 9;   3 + 6 = 9   and so on.

The yellow numbers also demonstrate the Commutative Property of Multiplication. You can multiply in any order; the product is the same.

2 x 9 = 9 x 2

Both equal 18.

x		1	2	3	4	5	6	7	8	9	10
0	0	0	0	0	0	0	0	0	0	0	0
1	0	1	2	3	4	5	6	7	8	9	10
2	0	2	4	6	8	10	12	14	16	18	20
3	0	3	6	9	12	15	18	21	24	27	30
4	0	4	8	12	16	20	24	28	32	36	40
5	0	5	10	15	20	25	30	35	40	45	50
6	0	6	12	18	24	30	36	42	48	54	60
7	0	7	14	21	28	35	42	49	56	63	70
8	0	8	16	24	32	40	48	56	64	72	80
9	0	9	18	27	36	45	54	63	72	81	90
10	0	10	20	30	40	50	60	70	80	90	100

Compare one row to another to find more patterns.

The numbers in the light blue row are double the numbers in the orange row. The numbers in the purple row are 3 times the numbers in the orange row.

The red diagonal line shows a pattern of square numbers. Each square number is the result of multiplying a number by itself, like

4 × 4 or **6 × 6**.

x	0	1	2	3	4	5	6	7	8	9	10
0	0	0	0	0	0	0	0	0	0	0	0
1	0	1	2	3	4	5	6	7	8	9	10
2	0	2	4	6	8	10	12	14	16	18	20
3	0	3	6	9	12	15	18	21	24	27	30
4	0	4	8	12	16	20	24	28	32	36	40
5	0	5	10	15	20	25	30	35	40	45	50
6	0	6	12	18	24	30	36	42	48	54	60
7	0	7	14	21	28	35	42	49	56	63	70
8	0	8	16	24	32	40	48	56	64	72	80
9	0	9	18	27	36	45	54	63	72	81	90
10	0	10	20	30	40	50	60	70	80	90	100

What's the Rule?

Let's make a rule. Choose the start number. Then tell how the numbers change.

Pattern rule: Start with 1. Multiply by 2. Continue multiplying by 2.

1, 2, 4, 8, 16, . . . ←——**multiplication pattern**

Start with 14. Continue adding 5.

14, 19, 24, 29, 34, . . . ←——**addition pattern**

Each number is called a **term**.

In an addition pattern, the numbers increase.

A multiplication pattern is called a **geometric** pattern. The numbers increase, but way more quickly!

If you have the rule, you can write the pattern.

Pattern rule: Start with 99. Continue subtracting 3. Write the first six terms.

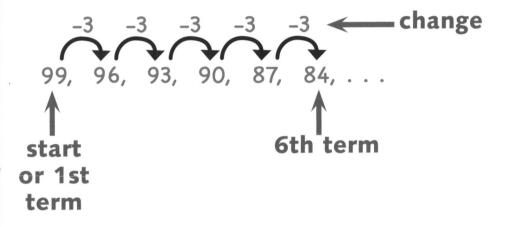

Use the rule:

Start with 13. Continue adding 3.

What are the first six terms?

If you don't have the rule, check how the numbers change.

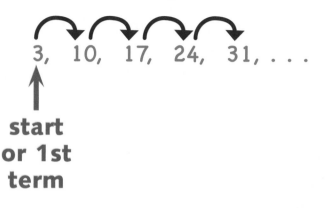

3, 10, 17, 24, 31, . . .

↑

**start
or 1st
term**

What change is there between the first term and the second term? +7

Think: 10 − 3 = 7   The rule could be add 7.

Check the changes between the other terms.
Is 10 + 7 = 17? **Yes**
Is 17 + 7 = 24? **Yes**
Is 24 + 7 = 31? **Yes**

Then you can extend the pattern. What is the tenth term?

3, 10, 17, 24, 31, □ □ □ □ □

Keep adding 7.   38 45 52 59 66

↑

10th term

a. What is the ninth term of the pattern?

1, 2, 4, 8, 16, . . .

b. What is the tenth term of the pattern?

4, 9, 14, 19, 24, . . .

c. What is the seventh term of the pattern?

2, 6, 18, 54, . . .

d. What is the eighth term of the pattern?

66, 69, ,72, 75, . . .

Other Pattern Rules

Some pattern rules involve two operations.

Addition and Subtraction

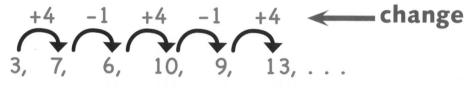

3, 7, 6, 10, 9, 13, . . .

Pattern rule: Start at 3. Add 4, then subtract 1. The next number is 12.

Try this one on your own.

8, 6, 12, 10, 16, 14, 20, . . .

Pattern rule:

Start at _____.

Subtract _____.

Add _____.

What are the next three numbers?

Answers: Start at 8. Subtract 2. Add 6.
The next three numbers are: 18, 24, 22

Multiplication and Addition

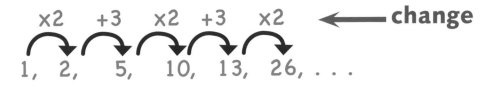

x2   +3   x2   +3   x2   ⟵ change

1,   2,   5,   10,   13,   26, . . .

Pattern rule: Start at 1. Multiply by 2, then add 3.

The next number is 29.

Try this one on your own.

2, 7, 14, 19, 38, 43, . . .

Pattern rule:

Start at _____.

Add _____.

Multiply by _____.

What are the next three numbers?

21

A picture helps you see this pattern.
Look at the change between the groups of
happy faces.

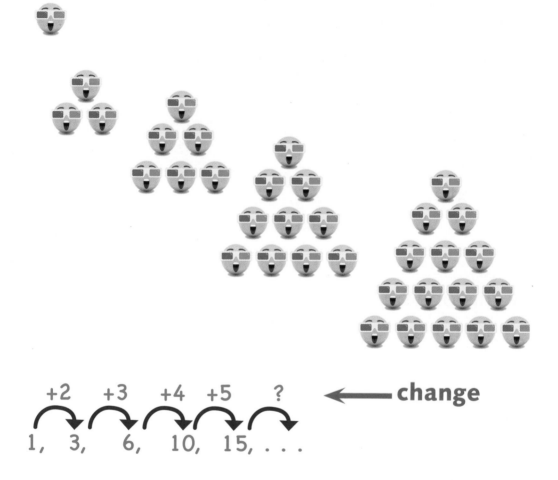

Pattern rule: Begin at 1. Add 2, then add 3,
then add 4, and so on. Add 1 more than you
added before to get each new term.

The next number in the pattern is 15 + 6 = 21

Just For Fun!

Look at this pattern that you can find in nature.

0, 1, 1, 2, 3, 5, 8, . . .

Pattern rule: Begin at 0. Add the two previous numbers to get the next number.

This pattern of numbers is the Fibonacci sequence. It describes the spiral arrangement of leaves on stems, petals on flowers, even the bumps on a pineapple, and much more.

Patterns Within Patterns

Sometimes there is a pattern in the terms.

These terms alternate even, odd, even, odd.

Start with 8. Continue adding 3.

8,   11,   14,   17,   20,   23, . . .

| even | odd | even | odd | even | odd |

These are all even.

Start with 10. Add 2. Continue adding 2.

10,   12,   14,   16,   18,   20, . . .

These are all odd.

Start with 9. Add 2. Continue adding 2.

9,   11,   13,   15,   17,   19, . . .

Look at the digits in the terms of a pattern to find other patterns.

The pattern is Multiples of 6.

6,   12,   18,   24,   30,   36, . . .

Add the digits in each term.

6	1 + 2	1 + 8	2 + 4	3 + 0	3 + 6
↓	↓	↓	↓	↓	↓
6	3	9	6	3	9

The sum of the digits in the terms form a pattern 6, 3, 9, that repeats.

Look at the multiples of 5.

5,   10,   15,   20,   25,   30, . . .

What other pattern do the terms show?

Comparing Two Patterns

Compare the terms in the same position. These are corresponding terms.

Term	1st	2nd	3rd	4th	5th	6th
Pattern A	2	4	6	8	10	12
	×4	×4	×4	×4	×4	×4
Pattern B	8	16	24	32	40	48

The numbers in Pattern B are 4 times the corresponding terms in Pattern A.

Analyze these patterns.

Term	1st	2nd	3rd	4th	5th	6th
Pattern C	5	9	13	17	21	25
	+5	+6	+7	+8	+9	+10
Pattern D	10	15	20	25	30	35

If you subtract the numbers in Pattern C from the corresponding numbers in Pattern D, the differences form the pattern

5,   6,   7,   8,   9,   10, . . .

Describe the rule for the pattern of differences between Pattern D and Pattern C.

Graphing Patterns

Use the corresponding terms of two patterns to make a graph.

Pattern X	1	2	3	4	5

Pattern Y	2	3	4	5	6

Turn the graphs around to make 2 columns. Then form **ordered pairs**.

Pattern X	Pattern Y	(X, Y)
1	2	(1, 2)
2	3	(2, 3)
3	4	(3, 4)
4	5	(4, 5)
5	6	(5, 6)

Patterns on a **Coordinate Plane**

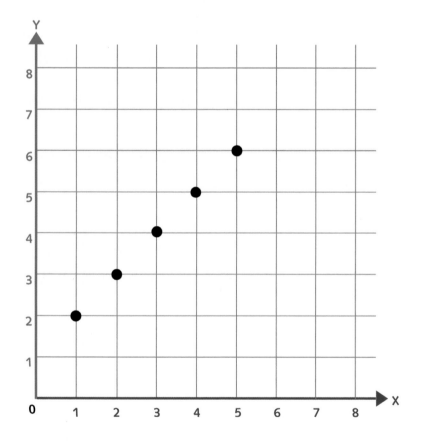

The points shown on the grid show a pattern too! One step right, one step up, and so on.

There are patterns all around you.

Glossary

coordinate plane (koh-OR-duh-nate PLAYN): a grid with two perpendicular number lines in which every point is associated with an ordered pair of numbers

core (kor) the smallest part of a pattern that repeats

even numbers (EE-vuhn NUHM-burz): numbers that can be divided exactly by 2. They will always have a remainder of 0.

geometric (jee-uh-MET-rik): of or having to do with geometry

odd numbers (ahd NUHM-burz): numbers that cannot be divided evenly by 2. They will always have a remainder of 1.

ordered pairs (Or-durd pairs): two numbers used to locate a point on a coordinate plane; the first number tells how far to move horizontally and the second number tells how far to move vertically

pattern (PAT-urn): a repeating arrangement of colors, shapes, and numbers

repeating pattern (ri-PEET-ing PAT-urn): a pattern in which the same set of numbers, shapes or colors are repeated

term (turm): each separate number in a pattern

Index

Websites to Visit

www.mathworksheets4kids.com/patterns.html
www.ixl.com/math/patterns
www.dadsworksheets.com/worksheets/number-patterns.html

About The Author

Claire Piddock lives by a pond in the woods of Maine with her husband and big dog, Otto. She loves painting landscapes, doing puzzles, and reading mysteries. She sees math as a fun puzzle and enjoys taking the mystery out of math as she has done for many years as a teacher and writer.

Meet The Author!
www.meetREMauthors.com

PHOTO CREDITS: Cover: lightbulb "brain" © Positive Vectors, emojis © CoolKengzz; Page 4 © espies, pages 6-7 © Erasdesign, page 8 dog and cat © Sarawut Padungkwan, page 11 © sunabesyou; page 22 © CoolKengzz, page 23 mint leaves © stockphotocatacart, flower © A. Trapulionis, pineapple © A. Trapulionis; page 26 © Ljupco Smokovski. All photos from Shutterstock

Edited by: Keli Sipperley

Cover and Interior design by: Nicola Stratford   www.nicolastratford.com

Library of Congress PCN Data

Patterns / Claire Piddock
(Math Masters: Analyze This!)
ISBN 978-1-68191-732-0 (hard cover)
ISBN 978-1-68191-833-4 (soft cover)
ISBN 978-1-68191-926-3 (e-Book)
Library of Congress Control Number: 2016932656

Rourke Educational Media
Printed in the United States of America, North Mankato, Minnesota

Also Available as: